# The Daily Don

## PANDEMIC EDITION

### FROM IMPEACHMENT TO IMBLEACHMENT

JESSE DUQUETTE

Arcade Publishing • New York

*For Leah, who always fights the power and does the right thing.*

Arcade Publishing books may be purchased in bulk at special discounts for sales promotion, corporate gifts, fund-raising, or educational purposes. Special editions can also be created to specifications. For details, contact the Special Sales Department, Arcade Publishing, 307 West 36th Street, 11th Floor, New York, NY 10018 or arcade@skyhorsepublishing.com.

Arcade Publishing® is a registered trademark of Skyhorse Publishing, Inc.®, a Delaware corporation.

Visit our website at www.arcadepub.com.

10 9 8 7 6 5 4 3 2 1

Library of Congress Cataloging-in-Publication Data is available on file.

Print ISBN: 978-1-951627-56-0
Ebook ISBN: 978-1-951627-61-4

Printed in the United States of America

# TABLE OF CONTENTS

# TWO-YEAR LOOK-BACK

Looking back at the first two years of this Administration, with its Kremlin debt and kids in cages, travel bans and tiki torches, it's hard not to feel like it all happened so much longer ago than it did. Of course, that could just be my terrible memory at work. I often forget things and when I am reminded of an event, it exists on a dubious time scale where something is just as likely to have happened last week as it could have in 1982. But when every passing day feels like a fortnight, and every week is a tour of duty, one could be forgiven for allowing the Roy Moores and Rocket Men to recede from consciousness into a distant past. Mueller and Stormy now seem like dusty curios, but not that long ago they were the Thing that might finally bring an end to our collective national nightmare, the bare patch on a dragon's belly waiting for an arrow. But, nope. No such savior was forthcoming, no deliverance in the third act. I had two years' worth of frustrated cartoons to look back upon and remind me of this fact, not that I needed it. And so I've continued to do as I have always done—drawing, drawing, always drawing—in the hopes that one day I might catch the moment when things turn and we can all take a breath.

   As of writing this, still waiting.

—Jesse Duquette

# 1

# SECOND VERSE, WORSE THAN THE FIRST

The second year of this presidency rolled into the third with all the distinction of a fifth marriage. There were the same ad-libbed make-'em-ups ("Windmill Cancer!") and jingoism ("Migrant Caravans!"), and the mere passing of time only seemed to embolden and exasperate the Base Whisperer's most base impulses. Spring came and went, and along with it any hopes that a long-awaited Report would save the day. By summer, Black and Brown congresswomen were being told to "go back" where they came from (Michigan? Minnesota?) and another massacre at the hands of a white supremacist was met with a presidential shrug. But something had begun to change. Maybe it was the neutering of the Mueller Report and what many had seen as an insurance policy against the Trump presidency. Maybe it was the deterioration of already-hideous conditions at the border and children crying for parents who would not be coming home, detained and deported while at work. Or, just maybe, it was that we had already seen a couple seasons of this show and we knew it was awful. How many reruns could we endure? Because, if there's anything more American than white supremacy and gun fetishism, it's an increasingly narrow attention span. And everything— the aberration of Trump, included—becomes old news someday.

February 9, 2019—White House physician says Trump is in "very good health" following his physical. Or, as I call it, "Anatomy of a Berder, With Cheese."

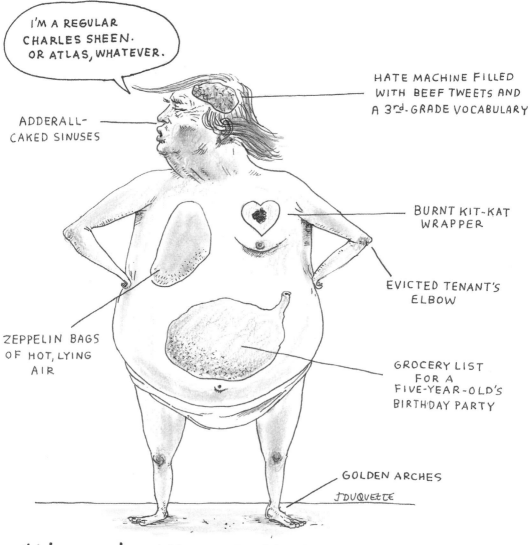

"We are healthy only to the extent that our ideas are humane." - Kurt Vonnegut

February 16, 2019—Trump bravely retreats to Mar-a-Lago during the scary national emergency of desperate families crossing the border, rudely trying to make a better life for themselves and their kids.

"Courage is found in unlikely places".
— J·R·R· Tolkien

"Violence is the last refuge of the incompetent."
— Isaac Asimov

March 22, 2019—Secretary Pompeo says Trump was "sent by God" to save the Jews, presumably from happy marriages and successful business ventures.

April 3, 2019—Trump claims wind turbines cause cancer. And why not? The same stable genius who brought you Nambia, eating pizza with a fork, and Eric Trump has to know what he's talking about, right?

"The fault lies not with the mob, who demands nonsense, but with those who do not know how to produce anything else."
— Miguel de Cervantes

April 18, 2019—Attorney General Barr applies more coverup than a flash sale at Sephora.

## BEFORE BARR

" THIS IS THE END OF
MY PRESIDENCY.
I'M FUCKED. "

         – DONALD J. TRUMP

## AFTER BARR

         – DONALD J. TRUMP

@the.daily.don

May 7, 2019—Ten years of Trump tax figures show over $1 billion in business losses over a nine-year period. Guess this dad-made thousandaire is to financial success what Mitch McConnell is to a strong jawline.

"You can't con people, at least not for long."
—Donald J. Trump

May 17, 2019—Republican lawmakers continue the push for God-drunk restrictions on a ~~witch's~~ woman's right to agency over her own body, mistresses and daughters excluded.

## UPDATED GOP LOGO

@the.daily.don

May 24, 2019—Unable to stomach putting a Black American on something as tremendous as money, Trump refuses to put Harriet Tubman on the $20 bill.

"Money doesn't talk, it swears."-Bob Dylan

# THINGS THAT GET
# UNDER DONALD'S SKIN

" 'NANCY', AS I CALL HER"

SYPHILIS

REVLON ® "PUMPKIN
PATCH" TONER

AUTO CORRECT

PEOPLE WHO WERE
CAPTURED

FREE RANGE MIGRANT
KIDS

JDUQUETTE

May 30, 2019—White House asks Navy to keep *USS John McCain* out of Trump's sight. Because when you're a fragile-spined shitbird, the dead rattle you like a grocery bag filled with stolen jewelry.

SOME ONE BETTER THROW A TARP OVER THAT SOCIALIST BROAD BY THE TIME I TURN AROUND OR I'M GONNA THROW THE MOTHER OF ALL TANTRUMS.

JDUQUETTE

"Our crime against criminals lies in the fact that we treat them like rascals."
— Friedrich Nietzsche

# THINGS MORE WELCOME IN LONDON THAN TRUMP

MISSPELLED
NECK TATTOOS

THE LUFTWAFFE,
1940

UNNECESSARY
COLONOSCOPIES

NIGEL
"MY MILKSHAKE BRINGS
ALL THE GITS TO THE YARD"
FARAGE

TESTICULAR
CANCER

THE REANIMATED
CORPSE OF
THERESA MAY'S CAREER
BEING SWARMED BY BEES

JDUQUETTE

June 4, 2019—Klu Kluxedo takes the "angry-at-my-clothes" look all the way to Buckingham Palace.

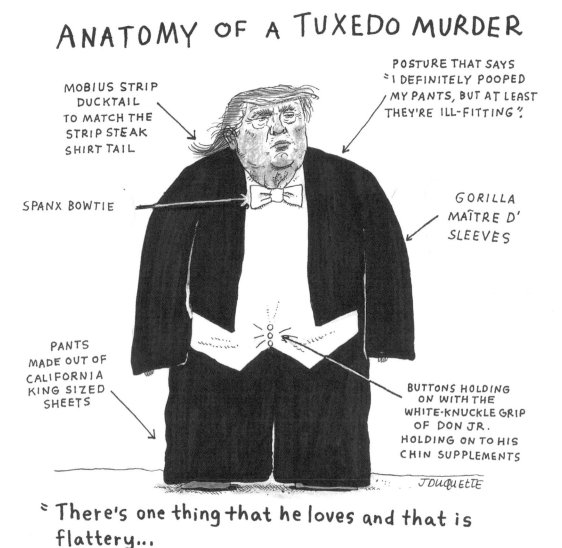

## ANATOMY OF A TUXEDO MURDER

MOBIUS STRIP DUCKTAIL TO MATCH THE STRIP STEAK SHIRT TAIL

POSTURE THAT SAYS "I DEFINITELY POOPED MY PANTS, BUT AT LEAST THEY'RE ILL-FITTING"

SPANX BOWTIE

GORILLA MAÎTRE D' SLEEVES

PANTS MADE OUT OF CALIFORNIA KING SIZED SHEETS

BUTTONS HOLDING ON WITH THE WHITE-KNUCKLE GRIP OF DON JR. HOLDING ON TO HIS CHIN SUPPLEMENTS

JDUQUETTE

"There's one thing that he loves and that is flattery...
'Cause he's a dedicated follower of fashion."
— Ray Davies

June 7, 2019—Trump forbids US embassies from flying Pride flags during Pride month. But not to worry, he's got a backup version up his Dorito-caked sleeve.

# TRUMP PRIDE FLAG

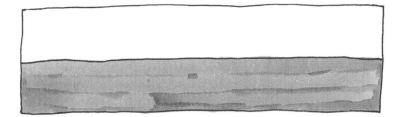

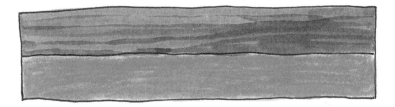

- WHITE, BECAUSE DUH

- BROWN FOR HAMBERDERS

- FLAG SEPARATED LIKE THOSE SHITHOLE FAMILIES

- BLUE FOR MIGRANT KID TEARS

- ORANGE FOR FAVORITE HUE OF "RACIST SUNSET" TONER

*@the.daily.don*

June 23, 2019—Let these names be as synonymous with the name "Trump" as Amber Alerts are with the name Roy Moore.

# FACES FROM
# DONCENTRATION CAMPS

JAKELIN AMEI
ROSMERY CAAL MAQUIN
AGE 7 yrs.

JUAN de LEÓN
GUTIERRÉZ
AGE 16 yrs.

CARLOS GREGORIO
HERNÁNDEZ VÁSQUEZ
AGE 16 yrs.

FELIPE GOMEZ
ALONZO
AGE 8 yrs.

WILMER JOSUÉ
RAMÍREZ VÁSQUEZ
AGE 2 yrs.

DARLYN CRISTABEL
CORDOVA-VALLE
AGE 10 yrs.

"We're doing a fantastic job."- Donald J. Trump

JDUQUETTE

June 29, 2019—Trump meets a fellow daddy issue–addled hair magician at the DMZ (probably thinking it was *TMZ*, if we're being honest).

"It is no wonder that we make terrible choices in our lives to avoid loneliness."
— Charles M. Schulz

July 5, 2019—Let us remember the brave soldiers who fought at the Battle of LaGuardia and wrested our independence from the British between baggage claim and the men's bathroom.

"Our army manned the air, it rammed the ramparts, it took over the airports..." - Donald J. Trump

July 10, 2019—Trump announces far-right social media summit. Think of it like a TED talk for Proud Boys who want to work out their Hillary feelings.

July 14, 2019—Trump tells Democratic Congresswomen of color to "go back" to the countries they came from. No word yet on how the nations of Michigan, New York, Minnesota, and Massachusetts will respond.

July 15, 2019—President Census Whitener must be real mad knowing these women will be around long after he's gone when the only mementos of him left will be traded on the dark web like Nazi bitcoin.

"It is unpatriotic not to tell the truth, whether about the president or anyone else."
– Theodore Roosevelt

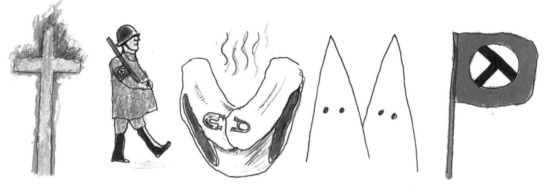

" What's in a name ? " - William Shakespeare

July 23, 2019—It always warms the heart when ferret-wigged turd merchants find each other.

"What does a mirror look at?"
– Frank Hebert

"If need be, save the presidency from the President."  — Richard M. Nixon

July 28, 2019—Chicken Littlehands shits on Baltimore because that's the presidential thing to do.

**CHARM CITY**　　　**BORN SHITTY**

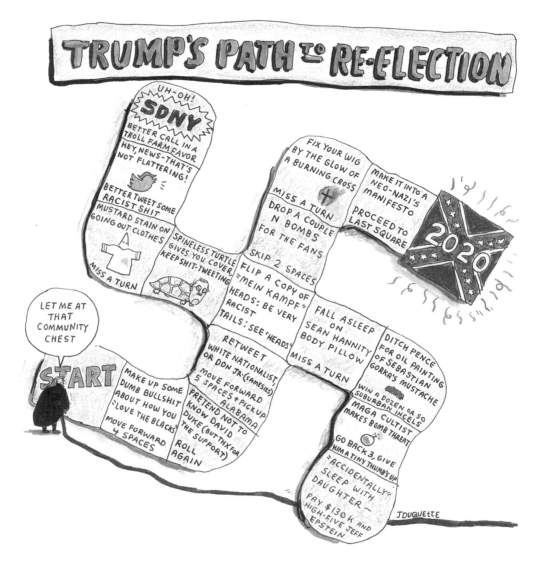

July 31, 2019—Newly released audio features Ronald Reagan being a total racist, as shocking as Eric Trump losing a spelling bee.

"I laugh at them because they're all the same."
— Kurt Cobain

August 6, 2019—More clockwork carnage from yet another mass shooting, this time in El Paso. And still, Mitch is as likely to do anything on gun control as he is to *not* win the gold in Committing Treason While Looking Like an Embarrassed Balloon.

August 7, 2019—Trump visits traumatized El Paso like a blundering bull in a gun-scarred china shop.

"We have no goodwill, no goodwill to give."
-David Berman

"It was only the Void pretending to be a man pretending not to know the Void." - Jack Kerouac

August 10, 2019—ICE goons raid several food processing plants, arresting hundreds and leaving many children suddenly orphaned. Or, as it's commonly called, "Stephen Miller-ing."

# 2019 = 1943

"Children come home from school to find that their parents have disappeared."
— Anne Frank

August 14, 2019

"If the Dow drops 1,000 points in two days
the President should be impeached immediately!"
                              — Donald J. Trump

"I don't want what we're doing to just end up as notes for a novel." — Ben Lerner

August 21, 2019

TRUMP CULTISTS: "HOW IS HE LIKE HITLER?"

TRUMP:

September 6, 2019—You can wash the ink off, but you can't wash the stink off.

# SHARPIEGATE

"You do it to yourself." - Thom Yorke

September 14, 2019—President Charm Vacuum reads the room, remembers he can't read, and takes on the public health crisis that's *really* on everyone's mind.

"No more guns for you." - Ross Macdonald

September 16, 2019—Grabby Wan Kenobi says the DOJ should "rescue" young Skyboofer from inconvenient claims of sexual assault.

# PERVS OF A FEATHER

| | |
|---|---|
| THINKS CONSENT IS FOR SUCKERS | CAN'T SPELL "CONSENT" |
| HAS FRIENDS WITH WEIRD NAMES LIKE "SQUEE" | HAS FRIENDS WITH WEIRD NAMES LIKE "JEFFREY EPSTEIN" |
| DRINKS UNTIL HE BLACKS OUT | WANTS TO KEEP THE BLACKS OUT |
| LOSES HIS COOL AROUND A STRONGER WOMAN | LOSES THE POPULAR VOTE TO A STRONGER WOMAN |
| SHOULD BE IMPEACHED | SHOULD REALLY BE FUCKING IMPEACHED |

# 2

# UKRAINE ALWAYS GET WHAT YOU WANT

I suppose when you're coming off of a summer filled with sharpie hurricanes, white supremacist shoot-'em-ups, and picking racist fights with Congresswomen, you've got to take stock of things and reflect. And to Trump, "reflect" means calling in a favor from your favorite papier-mâché–masked TV lawyer. Going from "America's Mayor" to "Treason's Major" is no easy feat, but I've got to hand it to Rudy for making the leap so boldly and unapologetically, like a golden retriever excitedly showing you he can catch bees in his mouth.

The ensuing months must have felt like wandering into a foreign film for Donald, all these alien-sounding words, words like "Zelensky," "Quid Pro Quo," and "illegal." And so rude! Two-and-a-half years of Making America Great Again, and people were still not speaking American. But these months were also not without some wins: we learned that phone calls can be "perfect," white evangelicals (still) love a bigoted fraud, and war criminals have a lot more time to attend your holiday parties when they've been disinvited from everyone else's.

Still, it must have come as a shock that sending your crime-comfortable consigliere abroad to dig up dirt like a trash-drunk possum and bribe a head of state in order to steal an election didn't go over well. Who could have guessed? I mean, it's not like wearing a tan suit or playing fast and loose with an email server or anything. But, whistles were blown, witnesses were called, and Matt Gaetz probably cried about something. And best of all, Donald gained a forever-gift from the whole impeachment hoax: a big scarlet asterisk next to the word "President*" in perpetuity, for all time, forever and ever.

September 20, 2019—Ever have one of those days when your meth-eyed tv lawyer job takes you overseas to do some shady shit for your criminal client, you're running around digging dirt like a grave-robbing ghoul, and all of a sudden it's treason time?

"Shady people do shady things."-
Steven Magee

@the.daily.don

" Don't do what Donny Don't does."- Bart Simpson

October 14, 2019—Happy Columbus Day from a murderous sailor and a lecherous failure.

HAD THE NINA, THE PINTA, AND THE SANTA MARIA

HAD THE MARLA, THE STORMY, AND THE KAREN McDOUGAL

FALSELY CREDITED WITH DISCOVERING NORTH AMERICA

FALSELY CREDITED WITH BEING A LEGITIMATE PRESIDENT

BROUGHT DISEASE TO INDIGENOUS PEOPLE

HAS ALL THE CHARM OF A SMALLPOX BLANKET

PRACTICED SLAVERY IN THE NAME OF THE QUEEN

ALLERGIC TO BRAVERY, THE SHAME OF QUEENS

"Smallpox champion US of A / Give natives some blankets / Warm like the grave."
— Fugazi

October 15, 2019—The album that's sure to hit the top of the "Music to Commit Many Crimes To" charts.

"Lawyers spend a great deal of their time shoveling smoke." - Oliver Wendell Holmes, Jr.

October 20, 2019—In which President Kremlin Debt's hangnail eyes can't see the writing on the wheel.

"Once you give a charlatan power over you, you almost never get it back." – Carl Sagan

October 22, 2019—Trump calls impeachment a "lynching," which makes sense coming from someone whose favorite strange fruit is master race orange.

October 25, 2019—In which a treason-curious dust mummy lawyer butt dials a reporter because that's what you do when you have all the cunning of a "Home Alone" burglar.

"It's about time law enforcement got as organized as organized crime."
— Rudy Giuliani

October 28, 2019—Friendless Urinal Cake takes in a ball game expecting synchronized Kim Jong fealty, gets blanketed by "boos" instead.

MAJOR LEAGUE BOOS

"Even Napoleon had his Watergate."
                    -Yogi Berra

November 1, 2019—Ivanka compares her daddy to Thomas Jefferson. I help her out with some of the similarities.

| | |
|---|---|
| OWNED SLAVES | OWNS THE GOP |
| FATHERED ILLEGITIMATE CHILDREN | FATHER TO ILLEGITIMATE ADULTS |
| ON THE $2 BILL | WORTH ABOUT $2 |
| REPRESENTATIVE IN THE CONTINENTAL CONGRESS | REPRESENTATIVE OF A CONTINENTAL BREAKFAST |
| PRINCIPAL AUTHOR OF THE DECLARATION OF INDEPENDENCE | PRINCIPAL AUTHOR OF THE DECLARATION OF IBS |
| WORE AN ODD WIG | SAMESIES |

November 4, 2019—The Quisling of Queens does his hometown a tremendous solid by packing up and absconding to the Sunshine State, where taxes are fiction and crazy is fact.

November 7, 2019—The Patron Saint of Axe Body Spray releases a book, coming soon to a Hobby Lobby clearance shelf near you.

"Books are the mirrors of the soul."
—Virginia Woolf

November 9, 2019—Polls show 63 percent of white Evangelicals don't believe Trump has hurt the dignity of the presidency. It's so cute when cults fall in love.

"Jesus wept." - John 11:35

November 15, 2019—Former US Ambassador to Ukraine Marie Yovanovitch gives her testimony about a sad bully whose impeachable offenses almost outpace his sexual assault allegations.

November 18, 2019—President Mayonnaise Sculpture undergoes a very tremendous "unplanned" physical, the closest he's ever been to the word "physical."

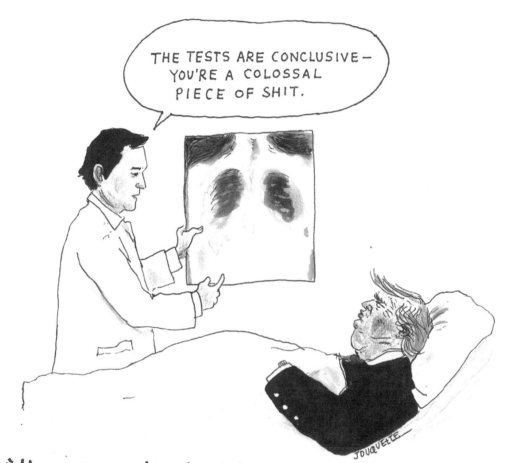

"He was a patient with a diagnosis that he couldn't understand." - Maggie Stiefvater

November 23, 2019—As the impeachment trial goes on, President Crime Champ's best boy goes dirt digging on the sly.

December 5, 2019—The only thing President Pariah Carey doles out more confidently than sick-burn nicknames are retweets of Nazis on Twitter.

# TRUMP'S NICKNAMES
## FOR HEADS OF STATE

**TWO-FACED**

**GERMAN FIVE**

**DÖNALDGANGER**

**KIMMY WITH
THE GOOD HAIR**

**A REAL CUT-UP**

**SIR**

"People try to make names for things they don't understand." - Rene Denfeld

December 13, 2019—Teenaged climate activist Greta Thunberg is named *Time Magazine's* "Person of the Year," proving the age-old adage, heck has no fury like a weak-kneed walrus scorned.

"I much prefer whining to counting my blessings." - Mary Ann Shaffer

# TRUMP'S FAVORITE BOOKS HE'S READ IN 2019

"I know words. I have the best words."
— Donald J. Trump

December 18, 2019—The House votes to give Trump access to a club so tremendously exclusive it only has three members.

"Show me a man with a tattoo and I'll show you a man with an interesting past."

\- Jack London

December 24, 2019—Trump hosts war criminal Eddie Gallagher at holiday parties because, well, no friends.

"It is better to be alone than in bad company."
- George Washington

December 25, 2019—Happy Holidays . . .

January 14, 2020—Giuliani lobbies White House to join impeachment defense team. And if there is anything I'd want to watch more than a tumbleweed-skinned, papier-mâché death-masked lawyer take part in the trial, I don't know what it is.

"Truth isn't truth." - Rudy Giuliani

January 19, 2020—Apologies to Jabba, Wavy Arm Guy, and pile of shit for involving them with a toddler-brained sleaze enthusiast.

January 20, 2020—For a forever-impeached Shithole President, MLK Day is just another non-descript, very untremendous Monday.

January 23, 2020—In which a kompromat-addled Kentuckian runs more interference than Michael Cohen cutting payoff checks.

"... he would not shrink from any act of servility if the need arose." – Marcel Proust

January 25, 2020—Trump's lawyers lay out their defense in closing statements so long I'm surprised Dumb Sauron didn't wear it as a tie.

"Bullshit is the glue that binds us as a nation."
- George Carlin

January 26, 2020—The Grand Wizard of Unearned Surname Privilege protects his nepotistic niche.

January 28, 2020—GOP Senators huddle on next steps in the impeachment trial like congressional cockroach cultists "deliberating" how best to put an end to daylight.

"A company of believers is like a prison full of criminals; their solidarity is based on what they can least justify about themselves."
—John Updike

January 30, 2020—Mitch and the gang do some soul searching as they prepare to block witnesses at their pageant trial.

"When you're a star, they let you do it."
— Donald J. Trump

February 1, 2020—Republicans crown their klannish king, just as word of a strange new flu comes from overseas. . . .

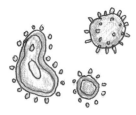

**CORONAVIRUS**

**CORONATION VIRUS**

"Sometimes I wish we could hear of a country that's out of Kings." — Mark Twain

# 3

# IRAN SO FAR AWAY (A DIGRESSION)

"But, wait a second!" you might say. "What better way to shake off the stink of impending impeachment than with some good, old-fashioned military aggression?" Not to worry, Herr Hair is way ahead of you. While typically reserving his ire for enemies of the state like Debra Messing and teenage climate activists, this time the beef-tweets were aimed at Iran and for a few days there it felt like we were on the verge of WWIII. And there was reason for concern; we'd already seen similar attempts to provoke baddies like North Korea and Baltimore into conflict. Who could say when Private Bone Spurs would make good on his sabre-rattling threats?

Thankfully, the whole thing fizzled out quicker than a Scaramucci* and all eyes were right back on a pageant masquerading as a trial. Sorry for the close call, world. Again.

*Scaramucci
*noun*   a unit of measurement equal to 10 days

"Cry havoc and let slip the dogs of war!"
-William Shakespeare

January 6, 2020—Very cool of Iran to spare the Tomb of the Unknown Hairline.

January 7, 2020—Iran launches more than a dozen missiles targeting US forces in response to Soleimani's assassination. Must be easy threatening war when you're far more likely to get caught hate-criming one of your undocumented servants than enlisting to serve your country.

"In order to get elected, Barack Obama will start a war with Iran."
—Donald J. Trump

January 10, 2020—President Narcisyphilis gets the cornered rat sweats over a Civil War daguerreotype spilling the beans on his "perfect phone call," says he'd use executive privilege to stop Bolton from testifying.

January 11, 2020—When your Defense Secretary was also a Raytheon lobbyist, everything is a target.

# 4
# WASH YOUR QUARANTEENY HANDS

It became evident that 2020 was the Voltron of Terrible Events within the first few days of February. In the span of a few short weeks, we had already endured impeachment, near-war by distraction, and Devin Nunes's face. The year was off to a supremely shitty start. But that was all very un-bigly compared to what was coming next, and the remarkable craziness that the Coronavirus would usher in.

The writing was on the wall right from the beginning, starting with Donald tapping Mike "Science is Satan" Pence to head the Coronavirus Task Force, apparently based on his handling of Indiana's HIV epidemic like a pilgrim battling witches. And, predictably, it only careened downward from there with downplayed deaths, "liberating" Michigan, and telling people to inject bleach. You know, the totally normal stuff that totally normal heads of states do in times of crisis.

It was also here that it seemed some of Bankruptcy Champ's bronzer bloom was finally coming off the rose—could it be his support was actually, ever-so-slightly waning? After all, it's hard convincing people something is a hoax if that hoax goes and kills your grandmother. But, if there's anything I've learned from documenting these past few years, it's that some people will go to any lengths—like, say, storming a state house over untimely haircuts—to show their undying devotion to a crappy cause.

February 2, 2020—Happy Groundhog's Day from a hate-curious Nazimodo.

"The shadow is me." - Anaïs Nin

February 26, 2020—Don't worry guys, the same game show grifter who thinks HPV is where you go to get your license renewed has this pandemic totally under control.

"The U.S. must immediately stop all flights from EBOLA infected countries or the plague will start and spread inside our 'borders'. Act fast!" – Donald J. Trump

February 27, 2020—When you think Coronavirus is just a fancy name for the Mexican Common Cold, you're bound to sleep on a pandemic or two.

February 28, 2020—Putting VP Pence in charge of the Coronavirus response is like putting Gov. Pence in charge of the AIDS response in Indiana—oh, wait.

From the desk of
Vice President
Mike Pence,
Coronavirus
Task Manager

## WAYS TO STOP CORONAVIRUS

- CONVERSION THERAPY

- TEN "HAIL MARYS" AND A PILGRIM HAT FILLED WITH HOLY WATER

- ONE OF MOTHER'S PATENTED FINGER-WAGS

- THROW IT IN A LAKE, SEE IF IT FLOATS

- GET SKY DAD TO SMITE IT LIKE HE DID WITH THE DINOSAURS A COUPLE HUNDRED YEARS AGO

- NICE TRY, SATAN — I KNOW THIS IS JUST A LIBERAL HOAX, LIKE EVOLUTION OR THE 21ST CENTURY

- THOUGHTS AND PRAYERS

"Smoking doesn't kill." - Mike Pence

@the.daily.don

February 29, 2020—I'm guessing President Lumbering Garbage Barge also thinks his tertiary syphilis is a hoax, because that dementia is settling in more comfortably than Don Jr. at a cross burning.

"On the throne of the world, any delusion can become fact." — Gore Vidal

J·DUQUETTE

March 4, 2020—Pestilential President = Presidential Pestilence.

# TRUMPANDEMICS

BANKRUPTCYPHILIS

QUID PRO CRABS

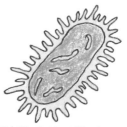

THE BUBONIC PUTZ

MAR-A-LAGONORRHEA

~~HIV~~
HPV
(OR IS IT DMV?)

ERIC

JDUQUETTE

March 5, 2020—Trump tells Americans to "go back to work" amidst a growing health emergency. Because if anyone knows about "work," it's the ferret-wigged freeloader who has spent 334 years of presidential salary (and counting) golfing at Mar-a-Lago on the taxpayers' dime.

# TRUMP EMERGENCY RESPONSES

JDUQUETTE

HURRICANES

WILDFIRES

GO BACK TO WORK, LOSERS

MASS SHOOTINGS

CORONAVIRUS

"If we have thousands or hundreds of thousands of people that get better, just by, you know, sitting around and even going to work, some of them go to work, but they get better." - Donald J. Trump

March 6, 2020—A microscopic task of astronomic importance.

March 9, 2020—Turning a disease into a dog whistle is the whitest of white power moves.

"CHINESE VIRUS"    SWINE FLU

March 10, 2020—President Turd Reich has a "natural ability" for pandemics in the same way Stephen Miller has a natural ability for not reflexively Sieg Heiling during normal conversation.

"There's none so blind as those who will not listen." – Neil Gaiman

March 11, 2020—Good news! Full Diaper has his very own sanitizer so now he can ride out this liberal pandemic cuckhoax safe and sound.

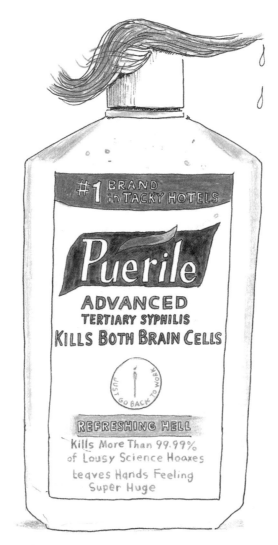

"I like this stuff. I really get it. Maybe
I have a natural ability." - Donald J. Trump

March 12, 2020—President Bankruptcy Champ makes sure his failing hotels and golf courses avoid the travel ban.

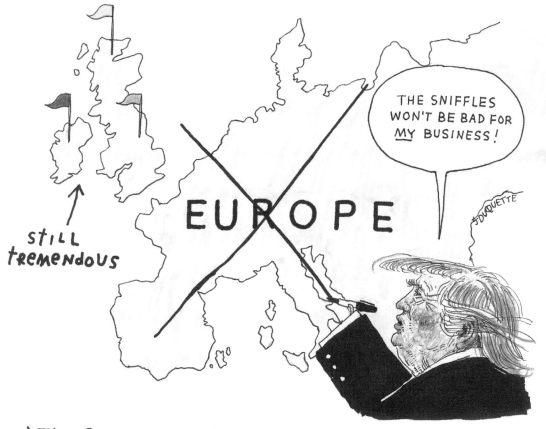

# TRUMP ANNOUNCES EUROPEAN TRAVEL BAN, STEERS CLEAR OF HIS STRUGGLING U·K· HOTELS, GOLF COURSES

THE SNIFFLES WON'T BE BAD FOR <u>MY</u> BUSINESS!

EUROPE

still tremendous

"The Coronavirus is very much under control in the USA... Stock Market starting to look very good to me." — Donald J. Trump

March 13, 2020—What happens when Sniffles the Science-Hating Clown runs the PPE show.

# MEDICAL MASKS

THE
PARTICULATE RESPIRATOR

THE
SURGICAL FACE MASK

THE
RESPIRATOR W/
VALVE

THE FACE SHIELD

THE
SURGICAL MOLDED

THE
TRUMP

March 14, 2020—This unwelcome plague disrupting everyone's lives is the pits. Coronavirus isn't so great, either.

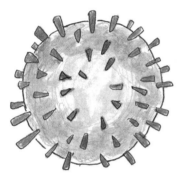

COVID-19

COVFEFE-45

JDUQUETTE

March 15, 2020—When you're President but also five years old and just drew on the family dog.

## TRUMAN

" THE BUCK STOPS HERE "

## FLUMAN

" I DON'T TAKE RESPONSIBILITY AT ALL "

JDUQVETTE

SOCIAL DISTANCING
MASK

Guaranteed to Repel!

March 17, 2020—Having a President during a pandemic who "didn't know people died from the flu" is like . . . well, having Donald Trump as your President.

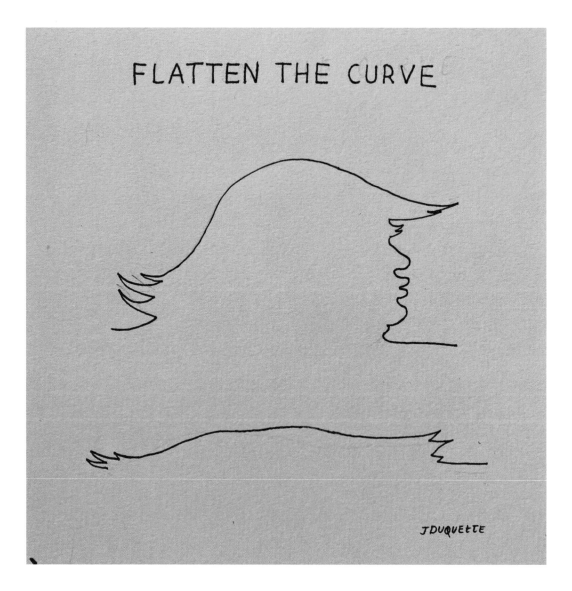

FLATTEN THE CURVE

JDUQUETTE

March 18, 2020—In which the Mickey Mouse Fan Club for Bigoted Frauds begrudgingly put their science pants on.

"I'm not an expert on the facts."
— Rudy Giuliani

March 19, 2020—The Quaransistine Chapel, socially distant.

March 20, 2020—Dr. Fauci does a killer impression of Americans for the past 1156 days.

March 21, 2020—When you've got some presidenting to do but toddler tantrums are so much more in your wheelhouse.

"You can tell the greatness of a man by what makes him angry." - Abraham Lincoln

March 22, 2020—In which the human equivalent of jury duty wishes very much you would all pretend he didn't say the things he very much said.

"He wears a mask, and his face grows to fit it."
— George Orwell

March 23, 2020—The More You Know But Definitely Don't Give A Shit About.

March 24, 2020—Greenbacks before Grandma, every time.

MAGA IN 1863

BUT WE _NEED_ SLAVERY FOR THE ECONOMY!

MAGA IN 2020

BUT WE _NEED_ TO WORK THROUGH A PANDEMIC FOR THE ECONOMY!

"When morality comes up against profit, it is seldom that profit loses."- Shirley Chisholm

March 25, 2020—Sociopath Distancing.

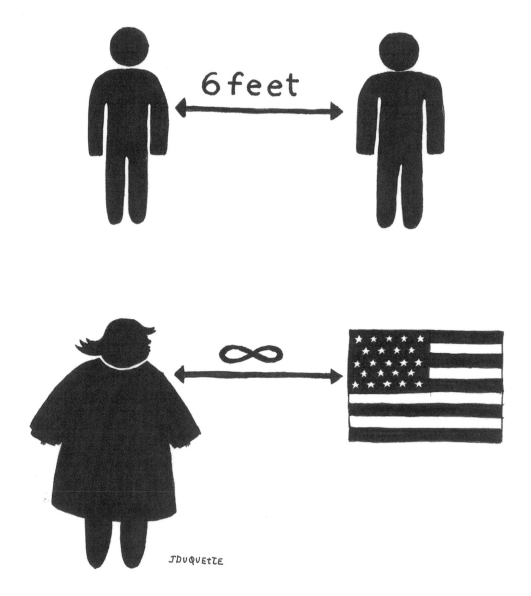

March 26, 2020—Fauci and Impeachi make their cases.

"Choose well. Your choice is brief, and yet endless." - Johann Wolfgang von Goethe

March 27, 2020—COVID cases in the US top 100K, the net result of giving pandemic preparedness the "we'll see what happens" treatment.

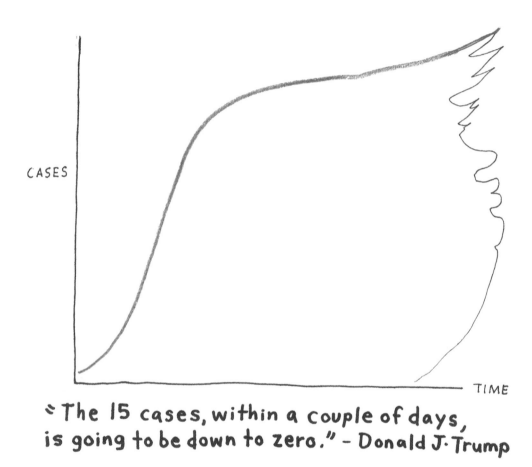

"The 15 cases, within a couple of days, is going to be down to zero." - Donald J. Trump

JDUQUETTE

March 28, 2020—The Patron Saint of Goofy Greaser Ducktails and Dick Tracy Villain Suits picks another fight with a woman he can't buy.

" WOMAN GOVERNOR "

SEX OFFENDER

Mar. 29th

March 30, 2020—If President Klan Chowder runs out of masks, he can always borrow one of Daddy's.

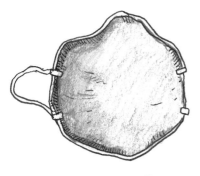

N95

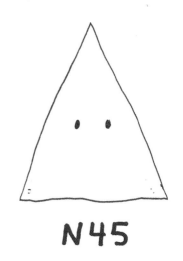

N45

JDUQUETTE

April 3, 2020—When the only things you know how to count are your bankruptcies and wives, what's a couple extra hundred thousand unnecessary deaths?

FEB 26th:
"THE 15 PEOPLE
WILL BE DOWN TO
ZERO IN A
COUPLE OF DAYS"

MAR. 29th:
200,000 DEATHS
WOULD BE A
"VERY GOOD JOB"

"We pretty much shut it down coming in from China." – Donald J. Trump

April 4, 2020—President Sex Offender tackles COVID-19 like it was a total "9."

"I alone can fix it." - Donald J. Trump

April 5, 2020—Trump says he won't wear a mask, for once a bigly decision on his part to take one for the team.

Donald J. Trump: 28M followers
Barack Obama: 53M followers
                          - Facebook

April 9, 2020—As US COVID deaths top 16K, President Empathy Void never misses an opportunity to be a real shit.

"The supreme vice is shallowness."
—Oscar Wilde

April 10, 2020—His true metric is sniffs per minute, but you say tomato, I say criminal failure.

April 11, 2020—President Summa Cum Fraude weighs whether or not to shut the country down because of a plague, his toughest call since deciding which brand of racist pumpkin toner to apply.

April 12, 2020—The United States sees the most COVID-related deaths in the world, but feeling #blessed to have a President with a "natural ability for this stuff." Otherwise we might have a pandemic on our tiny, tiny hands.

"The 15 cases within a couple of days, is going to be down to zero." - Donald J. Trump

April 14, 2020—When this is all over, let's not forget the weak-chinned Wormtongue who sat on his normal-sized hands while Dumb Sauron played President.

2020        3,500 B.C.

"It's allright if people think we are idiots.
It's all right if we open the coffin and
climb in."   – Robert Bly

DO COUGH ON ME

April 19, 2020—To be fair, the only test Public Access Caligula is guaranteed to ace is of the paternity variety.

"Donald Trump was the dumbest goddam student I ever had." - Prof. William T. Kelley

April 21, 2020—When you're riffing during a public health crisis and are also not very smart, sometimes you wind up telling people to drink some bleach. Normal stuff.

"I see the disinfectant that knocks it out in a minute, one minute."
— Donald J. Trump

"The two scents are much alike, as I recall."
– George R.R. Martin

April 23, 2020—'Merica means not having to say, "I'll listen to the advice of experts."

"Ignorance more frequently begets confidence than does knowledge."
— Charles Darwin

# HOW **NOT** TO WEAR A MASK

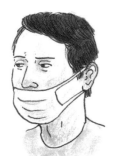

"Horror is the removal of masks."
    - Robert Bloch

April 26, 2020—Civil disobediencing while black vs. white.

SON OF A BITCH
TRAITOR

100%
PATRIOT

April 28, 2020—If there's one thing Trump loves more than lying about election fraud, it's engaging in it.

April 29, 2020—Pence goes mask-less during photo-op because rules are meant to be broken. Except for what you do in your slutty, slutty bedrooms, you Satan-rich Sodomites.

"Mike has a certain talent for this."
— Donald J. Trump

April 30, 2020—But did Bill Gates hire Mexican Bigfoot to cover up Pizzagate so no one would find out about Obama's plot to give white people cell tower chicken pox?

## THE FLU HOAX KLAN IN THE 18TH CENTURY

WELL, MY COUSIN SENT ME A YOUTUBE VIDEO THAT TOTALLY PROVES ELECTRICITY IS A GEORGIAN CUCKHOAX, SOOO, I'M GOING WITH THAT.

May 1, 2020—Maybe in Society 2.0 we should compensate the people who helped get us through this mess commensurate with how essential they have proven to be. You know, like professional athletes or hedge fund managers.

May 2, 2020—In which President Toddler Diet won't let an inconvenient hoax flu keep our tremendous meat cessplants from reopening! Viruses are just a spice, like mayo.

May 3, 2020—President Hospital Laundry barrels to reopening with the same proud disregard for science that brought us New Coke and goateed stormtroopers marching on state houses demanding to speak with the manager.

May 4, 2020—The GOP: when you wanna turn D-grade celebrities into politicians but also hate science and empathy.

May 5, 2020—Sure, Trump is telling people to inject bleach and he's using emergency funds to settle beefs and he doesn't know how to read and he gets his notions about medicine from 4chan chat rooms, but at least he didn't wear a tan suit like a Kenyan Muslim with all that fancy literacy and not acting like a colicky infant. Now THAT would be a real dealbreaker.

OBAMA'S
TAN SUIT

>

TRUMP'S
WHITE SUIT

@the.daily.don

May 7, 2020—If COVID tests are "beautiful" and phone calls are "perfect," then, sure, gun-fetishizing, science-allergic aspirational Rambos storming state capitols are "very good people."

"You have to quit confusing a madness with a mission." - Flannery O'Connor

May 8, 2020—Thoughts and prayers to Pence's spokeswoman and ghoul enthusiast Katie Miller for testing positive for COVID. Just have your hubby run down to the pharmacy to pick you up a handle of bleach—what have you got to lose?

"... I will encounter darkness as a bride, and hug it in mine arms."
— William Shakespeare

May 11, 2020—Don't worry about the totally hoax-y body count. President Traitor the Hutt has done such tremendous prevailing the likes of which no one has ever prevailed before, we're all gonna get sick of prevailing.

# OBAMAGATE

May 16, 2020—Practice what you bleach.

May 17, 2020—In which Dr. Bright and President Blight differ on the merits of chugging a rack of bleach very strongly, very tremendously, everyone is doing it.

"Great is the power of steady misrepresentation." – Charles Darwin

# THE ULTIMAGA SACRIFICE

"I think by Memorial Day weekend we will have this Coronavirus epidemic behind us." — Mike Pence

May 22, 2020—"I tested very positively in another sense. I tested positively towards the negative, right? So no, I tested perfectly this morning. Meaning I tested negative. But that's a way of saying it. Positively toward the negative."— President Donald Trump, 5/21/2020

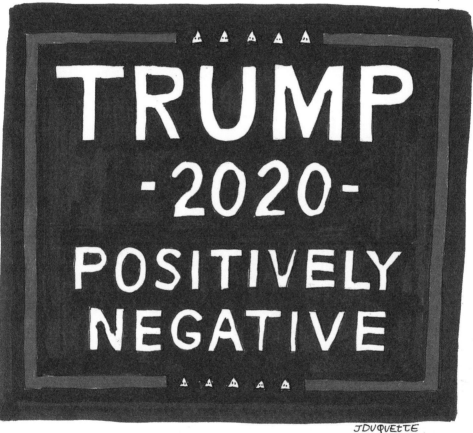

May 23, 2020—President Body Count Enthusiast hopes to pack the pews like it's the federal judiciary.

May 24, 2020—Why, yes, 100,000 dead Americans does seem like a good time for a Virus Death Champ to take a load off from beef-tweeting and pill-popping to cheat his way through a round of golf or five.

"Barack Obama plays golf to escape work while America goes down the drain."
— Donald J. Trump

May 24, 2020

MEMORIAL DAY
WEEKEND
**100K DEAD**

FEB. 26ᵀᴴ

"THE 15 CASES,
WITHIN A COUPLE
OF DAYS, IS GOING
TO BE DOWN
TO **ZERO**."

"It will take time to restore chaos."
- George W. Bush

May 25, 2020—President Ass Menagerie reserves his "fire and fury" for only the most bigly of emergencies, like brown people voting and journalists asking questions.

100K COVID
DEATHS

MASS SHOOTINGS

HURRICANES

WHITE SUPREMACY

WILDFIRES

ELECTION MEDDLING

FAILED HEALTHCARE
SYSTEM

@the.daily.don

CLIMATE CHANGE

HURT FEELINGS
ON TWITTER

May 26, 2020—"Unknown Soldier?" Seems pretty untremendous honoring someone who, like, doesn't even have any Twitter followers. But at least the cameras are rolling.

"I think I've made a lot of sacrifices."
— Donald J. Trump

# 5
# EIGHT MINUTES, FORTY-SIX SECONDS

The protests that unfolded in the wake of George Floyd's murder were not a by-product of anti-Trump fervor. After all, it wasn't his knee on a Black man's neck for eight minutes and forty-six seconds. Just as with COVID-19, the Black Lives Matter movement could never be reduced to a single person or policy and eclipsed even Trump, an anthropomorphized insecurity blanket used to being the center of attention. For once, to paraphrase William Martin Joel, he didn't start the fire. But, just as with COVID-19, he turned a stovetop burner into a forest fire and made a bad situation much, much worse. The echoing of '60s-era supremacist slogans, the tear-gassing of protestors for a tiny-handed bible photo op, the reliable dog-whistling about "thugs"; all of it served to prove what we already knew: that the bigot in bronzer was as uniquely unqualified to rise to the moment as he was to successfully walk down a ramp.

May 21, 2020—Looking forward to the day when white people are as outraged over modern-day lynchings as they are with not getting their nails done.

## 1955

### EMMETT TILL

KILLED FOR LOOKING
AT A WHITE WOMAN
WHILE BLACK

## 2020

### AHMAUD ARBERY

KILLED FOR JOGGING
BY WHITE PEOPLE
WHILE BLACK

May 27, 2020—As American as apple pie and conflating inconvenience with tyranny.

# 1 COUNTRY, 2 SYSTEMS

### GEORGE FLOYD
SUSPECTED OF "FORGERY",
KILLED BY POLICE

### DYLANN ROOF
MURDERED 9 PEOPLE,
ARRESTED PEACEFULLY

"We were murdered so often, I started believing Black bodies made better fertilizer." – Darnell Lamont Walker

BENEFIT      DOUBT

JDUQUETTE

May 29, 2020—It was never about standing during a song. It was never about disrespecting veterans. It was always about our country's never-ending open season on black and brown people.

# PROBLEMS

I WANT TO SPEAK
WITH THE MANAGER

I CAN'T BREATHE

JDUQUETTE

May 31, 2020—400+ years of structural oppression and systemic racism vs. two months of having to wear a mask and stay indoors.

TEAR GAS          FREE PASS

June 1, 2020—For a country whose foundational currency was black bodies in bondage, these lynchings will always be a feature, not a flaw.

"Because the machine will try to grind you into dust, whether or not we speak."
— Audre Lorde

June 3, 2020—Objects in the rearview mirror of history are larger than they appear.

June 4, 2020—President Baby Whisper Skin shows Governors how not to be "weak" by hiding out in his bunker like my dog during some light thunder.

"Hatred is the coward's revenge for being intimidated." - George Bernard Shaw

June 5, 2020—Do we have Hitler Bingo yet if we've got someone who hides in a bunker and gasses his people?

"There is freedom of speech, but I cannot guarantee freedom of speech." - Idi Amin

June 7, 2020—As long as we're dismantling anachronistic monuments to bigotry, let's make this a one-term presidency.

June 9, 2020—Systemic racism is bad and all, but have you heard about untimely haircuts?

June 15, 2020—White supremacist pigeon toilets are the Eric Trump of heritage.

"To me they're just rock shaped into glorious nobodies." - Chuck Palahniuk

June 16, 2020—Big ask, but maybe, just maybe, the right of a Black man to not be killed by police for sleeping in his car should be respected at least as much as the right of a Nazi in custody to have his quarter-pounder.

June 22, 2020—Macaulay Sulkin' mopes his way back from a Tulsa rally attended by an audience of dozens, but he'll always have the Aryan albatross around his neck to keep him company.

"Orange is the colour of despair, and pumpkins."
– Cassandra Clare

# 6

# CALAMARI LIPS SINK SHIPS

All summer long the hits kept coming. Revelations of Russian bounties on US troops prompt the White House press secretary to declare the President "the most informed person on planet Earth." The DOJ fires prosecutors investigating Trump while criminals are pardoned and sentences are commuted. How could an entire crappy lifetime spent rampantly crime-ing under the protection of subterranean cronies and hush money payoffs continue to go unpunished? What cosmic night-mare deal was brokered that allowed for such untouchability? As it turns out, the cornered-rat prison sweats aren't a good look—even on a stable genius—and the desperation brought on by an ever-nearing election really made this money-baked ham perspire.

The pandemic raged on, relentlessly and without surprise. Only this time, it was the *South* with ICU bed envy and Bronx-level COVID cases. Arizona, Alabama, Florida. This was Trump country. His biggest gamble to date in telling the faithful that the Coronavirus was an irrelevant hoax was not paying off as planned, but instead underscored the sad fact that he was as capable of managing a health crisis as he was of officiating a dog funeral. The choppy waters of his presidency were getting a whole lot choppier, and some of the less-faithful began to jump ship. Every presser belted out in half-words under the din of Marine One, every self-immolating beef-tweet only did more damage until finally, at long last, it seemed the boat had sprung a leak.

They say shit floats, but I couldn't help feeling a sense of comfort that after all this time, it wasn't the "Deep State" doing him in as he brought the Klan to the Ku Klux; cratering polls could not be blamed on Fake News while he persisted in virus magical thinking. No, this time, the dishwater-haired dunderpate was sinking himself.

June 26, 2020—A beloved record turns thirty, and a belligerent presidency turns a gazillion. At least, that's how it feels watching military fetishists twist themselves into fawning pretzels trying to explain Bone Spurs ignoring Russian bounties on US troops.

June 27, 2020—Very much looking forward to hearing how it was Obama's fault that Trump rolled over like a love-starved puppy and gave the syphilis shrugs upon finding out Putin has been putting prices on the heads of soldiers overseas.

July 2, 2020—I suppose it's less than surprising to hear President Nocabulary doesn't know how masks work, given his track record with umbrellas, bottles of water, and running successful businesses.

"I look like the Lone Ranger."
- Donald J. Trump

July 8, 2020—SCOTUS does religious zealotry a solid by ruling employers have a say in their employees' health and birth control choices because, well, Bronze Age bedtime stories and lady-hating.

MY BODY,
MY CHOICE

YOUR BODY,
MY CHOICE

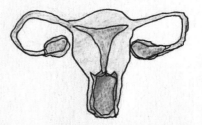

JOUQUETTE

July 10, 2020—With so many prison-ready crimes waiting for him once he's out of office, news that Donny's matchmaker friend is ready to name names is just one sapling in a felonious forest.

July 12, 2020—Regrettable Steampunk Embarrassment Roger Stone has his sentence commuted for being a dutiful stooge. I doubt anyone will offer President Resting Crime Face the same treatment as he's being shuffled down a ramp to the Hague.

### KALIEF BROWDER

WRONGFULLY ACCUSED OF STEALING A BACKPACK

JAILED FOR 3 YEARS ON RIKER'S ISLAND AT 16 YRS OLD, 2 YRS IN SOLITARY

KILLED HIMSELF AFTER ENDURING BRUTAL, ABUSIVE TREATMENT

### ROGER STONE

CONVICTED OF WITNESS TAMPERING, OBSTRUCTION, LYING TO CONGRESS

SENTENCED TO 3 YEARS, TRUMP COMMUTES SENTENCE

DOESN'T SPEND ONE NIGHT IN PRISON

JDUQUETTE

"The President does read."